JAPAN

By Charis Mather

All rights reserved.
Printed in Poland.

A catalogue record for this book is available from the British Library.

ISBN: 978-1-80155-587-6

Written by:
Charis Mather

Edited by:
William Anthony

Designed by:
Drue Rintoul

©2022
BookLife Publishing Ltd.
King's Lynn, Norfolk
PE30 4LS, UK

All facts, statistics, web addresses and URLs in this book were verified as valid and accurate at time of writing. No responsibility for any changes to external websites or references can be accepted by either the author or publisher.

Image Credits

All images are courtesy of Shutterstock.com, unless otherwise specified. With thanks to Getty Images, Thinkstock Photo and iStockphoto.

Cover – julianne.hide, Guitar photographer. 2–3 – TNShutter. 4–5 – Matis75, Wathanachai Janwithayayot. 8–9 – Neale Cousland, Sean Pavone. 10–11 – Zallaz, MADSOLAR. 12–13 – Navapon Plodprong, soi7studio. 14–15 – Rido, pang_oasis. 16–17 – JenJ_Payless, oneinchpunch. 18–19 – Sean Pavone, Natapat2521. 20–21 – cowardlion, vichie81. 22–23 – Wissuta.on, Nonthachai Saksri.

CONTENTS

Page 4   Country to Country

Page 6   Today's Trip Is to... Japan!

Page 8   Tokyo

Page 10   Mount Fuji

Page 12   Hanami

Page 14   Japanese Food

Page 16   Tea Ceremony

Page 18   Animal Parks

Page 20   Trains

Page 22   Before You Go...

Page 24   Glossary and Index

Words that look like this can be found in the glossary on page 24.

COUNTRY TO COUNTRY

Countries are areas of land and the people that live there. Different countries usually have their own rules and ways of living. Countries usually have clear **borders** that are drawn on maps.

What country do you live in?

The world is full of countries. Each country has its own interesting places and people. What country will we visit in this book?

How many countries can you name?

TODAY'S TRIP IS TO...
JAPAN!

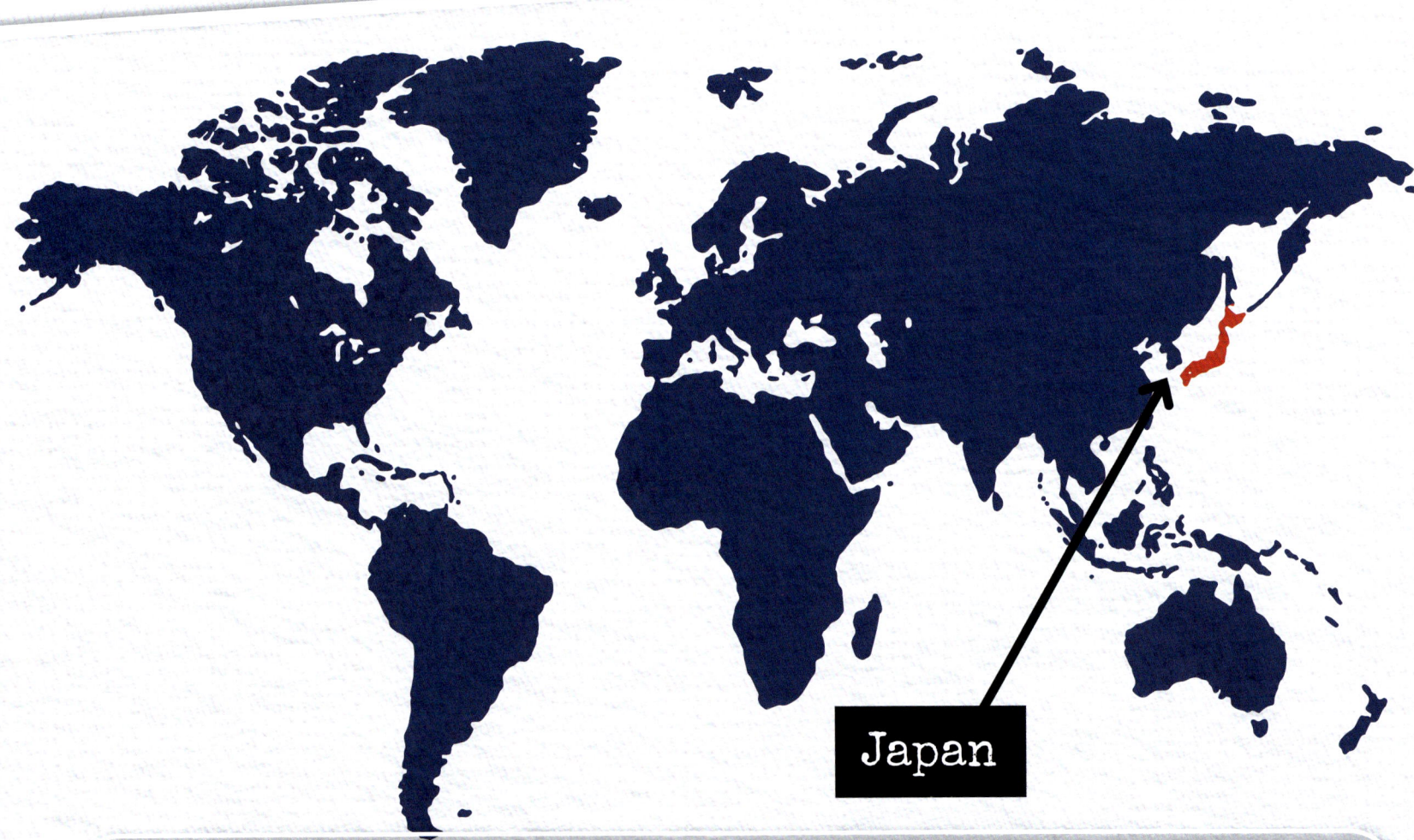

The country of Japan is in a part of the world called Asia. Asia is a continent, which is an area of land made up of lots of countries. Can you see Japan on the map?

FACT FILE

Capital city: Tokyo
Main language: Japanese
Currency: Yen
Flag:

Currency is the type of money that is used by a country.

TOKYO

We are in Tokyo, the capital city of Japan. Here, you can see Tokyo Tower. Tokyo Tower is over 300 metres tall. It is easy to see because of its red colour and lights.

You can sometimes see Japan's most famous mountain from Tokyo Tower.

Shibuya Crossing is one of the busiest crossings in the world.

Tokyo is a very busy city. Many people get to work each day by going over Shibuya Crossing. Thousands of people cross the big roads outside of the train station every few minutes.

MOUNT FUJI

Many people who visit Tokyo also come to see Japan's highest mountain. Mount Fuji is a type of mountain called a **volcano**. You can see snow at the top during winter.

It can take five to ten hours to climb Mount Fuji.

Mount Fuji is very important to many Japanese people, especially followers of **Shinto**. People who climb the mountain might see **shrines** on the way.

HANAMI

In the spring, many people enjoy looking at beautiful cherry blossom trees together. Each year, friends and families meet outside to have picnics under the trees. This is called hanami.

Hanami means 'flower watching' in Japanese.

Blossoms might only be around for 10 to 14 days.

Cherry blossom trees only have flowers for a short time. During hanami, people watch flower **petals** falling from the trees. Sometimes this makes it look like it is snowing.

JAPANESE FOOD

If you go to Japan, you might get to try many fresh **seafood** dishes. Some dishes, such as sushi and sashimi, are made from **raw** fish. Japanese food often includes rice.

You can find other types of food at Japan's outdoor food stands, called yatai. Yatai are open in the evenings. They can also be moved around. Food is cooked at the yatai and eaten straight away.

Yatai serve dumplings, grilled chicken, noodles and much more.

TEA CEREMONY

Tea is a common drink in Japan, but there are also special **ceremonies** where tea is made to welcome guests. In tea ceremonies, the drink is **prepared** very carefully.

Tea ceremonies can last for many hours.

Guests sit quietly on the floor while the tea is prepared. There are many steps and tools needed to make it. Once the tea is ready, the guests wait to drink it one at a time.

The tea ceremony is a very peaceful event.

Animal Parks

Jigokudani Park

In some parts of Japan, you can see monkeys in the wild. Jigokudani Park is also called Snow Monkey Park because of the monkeys that live there. They often sit in pools of water.

In the city of Nara, there is a park that has hundreds of deer. The deer are used to seeing people and will sometimes let visitors feed them.

Nara Park

TRAINS

In Japan, speaking on the phone while on the train can be seen as rude.

Japan's trains are known across the world for being on-time. They are also very quiet inside, even though many people travel on them. Japanese people try not to disturb other people around them.

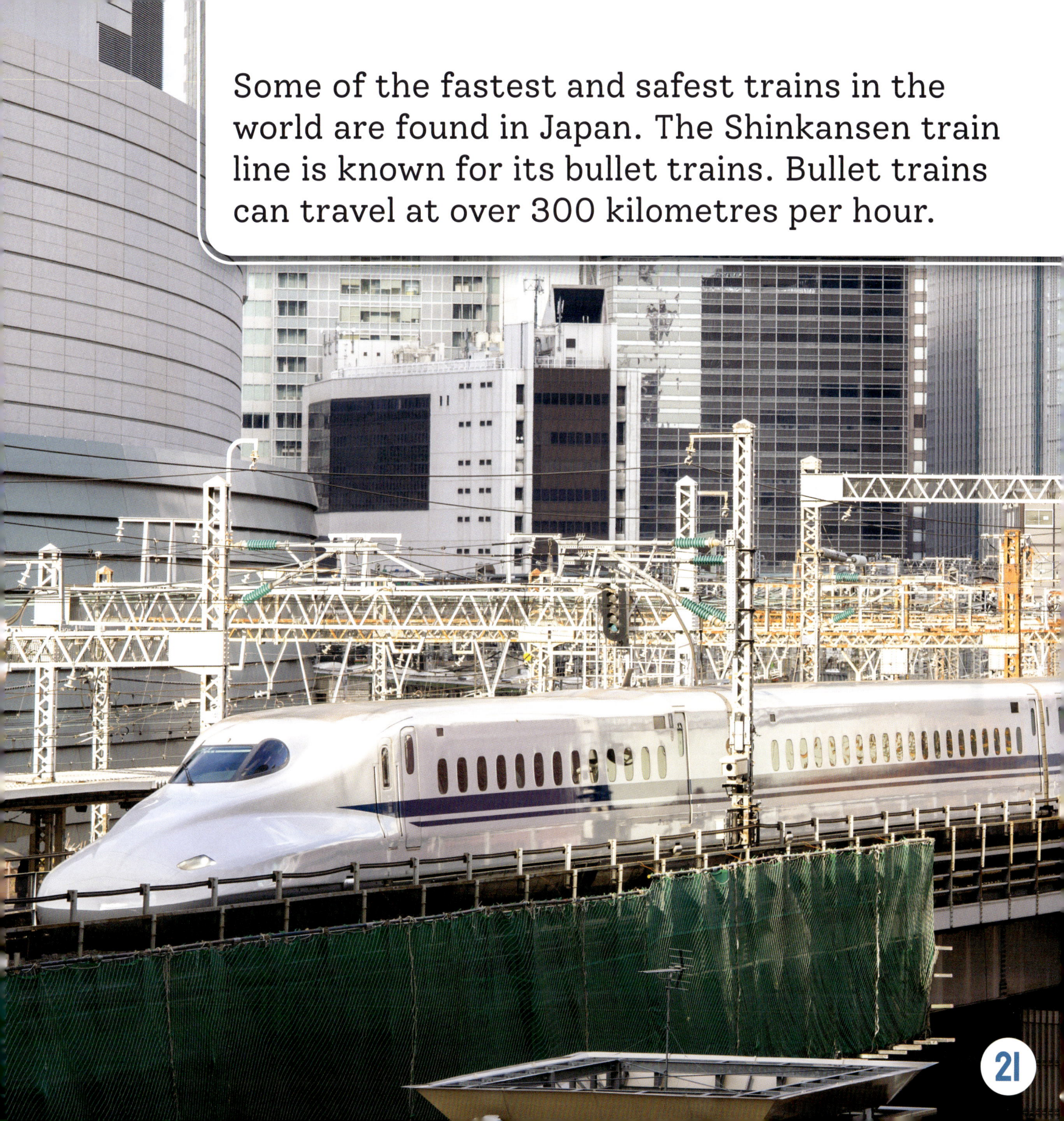

Some of the fastest and safest trains in the world are found in Japan. The Shinkansen train line is known for its bullet trains. Bullet trains can travel at over 300 kilometres per hour.

BEFORE YOU GO...

Many people go to visit the Fushimi Inari shrines. Visitors can walk through thousands of bright red Shinto shrines. If you visit, make sure to look out for the fox statues near the shrines.

If you go to Osaka, make sure to see Osaka Castle. It was first built by one of Japan's **samurai** rulers. There is lots to learn about Japan's history at Osaka Castle.

What have you learnt about Japan today?

GLOSSARY

borders	lines that show where one place ends and another begins
ceremonies	events that are done in the same way each time and have meaning to the people involved
petals	the colourful leaves that make up a flower
prepared	made ready
raw	not cooked
samurai	people who were in charge of ruling and fighting many years ago in Japan
seafood	animals from the sea, such as fish or crabs, that are served as food
Shinto	a Japanese religion where nature and family are important
shrines	a place that is built to honour and remember an event or being
volcano	a mountain that can form from hot gas and melted rock, which is called lava

INDEX

castles 23
deer 19
monkeys 18
mountains 8, 10–11
shrines 11, 22
snow 10, 13, 18
Tokyo 7–10
trees 12–13